Honoré Daumier

A Collection of His Social and Political Caricatures
Together with an Introductory Essay on His Art

By

Elisabeth Luther Cary

——————

With Seventy-six Illustrations

——————

G. P. Putnam's Sons
New York and London
The Knickerbocker Press
1907

The Knickerbocker Press, New York

ILLUSTRATIONS

Illustrations

Honoré Daumier

Honoré Daumier

I F we care to look upon the France of the past century through eyes that note not merely the surface view, but types, characteristics, deep-seated principles, unconscious tendencies, with a clear appreciation of their values and relations, we cannot do better than turn page by page a collection of Daumier's drawings, if by good fortune such may have fallen in our way. The chances are that our social and political ruminations will, however, be somewhat disturbed, and at times overwhelmed, by the extraordinary beauty of the art thus unfolded. Whether we are contemplating a "bas-bleu," a Robert Macaire, a Bohemian of the Paris streets, an amateur of art, a barrister, a bourgeois family, or a statesman, we are confronted by the same magnificent vitality of line, the same exquisite modulations of light and shade, the same massive structure and clear definition of form. The artist's sense of sheer fun, his willingness to lash political opponents, his discerning eye for temperamental and moral traits, unquestionably are elements in our enjoyment; but nothing counts as

much as the æsthetic charm.   By this Daumier's art ranks
with that of the masters, and conclusively demonstrates,
if demonstration were needed, that the "subject" and the
"literary" interest of a picture as little impair as improve
its pictorial value.

Honoré Daumier was born at Marseilles on the twenty-
sixth of February, 1808, and by the time he was twenty-
one had commenced his career as a lithographer. His
education in art had been, apparently, of the slenderest
description, but had been supplemented by long strolls
through the galleries of the Louvre, especially in the department of antiques, where, no doubt, classic simplicity
and breadth had their effect upon his vision, enabling him,
after the fashion of great art, to perceive these qualities
in the world of multitudinous detail surrounding him.
Chance brought him into relations with a lithographer who
taught him his trade, and by the time he was twenty-one
he was working, for the most part anonymously, for a pub-
lisher by the name of Béliard, and presently for Ricourt,
Hautecœur-Martinet, and, most important of all, for
Charles Philipon and the house of Aubert.

It is difficult to recognise in his beginnings the presage of
his robust genius. He notes expression and detail, but is
feebly uncertain in his composition, and his lights and
shadows are scattered over the space like a brood of fright-
ened chickens without organisation or intention. In the
admirable *catalogue raisonné* of the lithographs, edited by

Mm. Hazard and Delteil, the earliest known lithograph is tentatively ascribed to 1829. This represents a fatuous old man (Mayeux) seated between two ambiguous charmers who are plying him with champagne. In the background is a maid leaving the room with a bottle and a plate in her hands. The drawing is weak and indeterminate, and the values are practically non-existent so far as any logical relation between them is concerned; yet the picture manages to convey the artist's meaning with singular directness. The sly and senile smile on the face of the flattered old man, the awkward coquetry of the large woman on his left, the contrast between his shrunken frame and the abounding contours of his companions, might have been found on a page of Thackeray's Sketch-Book. The subject certainly is one that would have appealed to the English satirist; and it is not one that is characteristic of Daumier's choice.

The following year the political weekly entitled *La Caricature* was founded by Philipon with the artistic collaboration of Daumier, Grandville, Despéret, Monnier, Decamps, Raffet, Traviès, Bouquet, Benjamin Roubaud, and others. From the beginning of 1832 Daumier played an active part in connection with this publication, contributing to it from first to last no fewer than a hundred lithographs. The earlier ones were signed with the pseudonym, *Rogelin*, and were without especial distinction of execution. They were drawn, to use M. Champfleury's words, as a child draws from casts. One, signed H. Daumier, published prior to

August 30th, 1832, and entitled *Gargantua*, represents
Louis-Philippe seated on his throne and swallowing bags
of coin which have been extracted from the poor by his
ministers, and which are carried by lilliputian personages
up a plank that stretches from the ground to his mouth.
At the foot of the plank is a crowd of miserable men and
women handing over their money. About the throne are fat
little favourites gathering up peerages, decorations, com-
missions, and the like, into which the enforced offerings have
been converted. Here still the drawing is to the last degree
immature, the only suggestion conveyed by it of the later
richness and solidity of Daumier's work appearing in the good
round contour of Louis-Philippe's heavy body, pendent over
his small legs.　The satiric intention, however, was sufficient
to throw the artist into prison, where he remained from
September, 1832, to February, 1833, accumulating, apparently, a fine store of antipathies toward judges, juries,
and barristers that were to form the basis of a remarkable
series of drawings and a few paintings in which his genius
reaches its high-water mark.　For two and a half years after
his release—until *La Caricature* was stopped by the restric-
tion of the liberty of the press—he produced work in which
a certain ferocity of moral conviction and ardent youthful
vengeance against social evils, found expression in blacks
and whites and greys marshalled and ordered for his artistic
purposes with the firmest authority.　He was now in full
possession of his instrument and able to support his intel-

lectual idea with his ripened craftsmanship. One of the most beautiful products of this period is the famous figure of Barbe-Marbois, the nonogenarian marquis, seated in his arm-chair, his quilted gown wrapped about his withered limbs, his head in its close black cap drooping forward, his hands, gnarled and thin, passively crossed, his mouth partly open, his pale profile sharply cut—a wonderful representation of extreme age without a feature compromised or softened, yet keeping by the unity and force of the workmanship a superb dignity, the unimpeachable gravity of great art.

A composition directly reflecting Daumier's own experience is the lithograph entitled *Souvenir de Ste. Pélagie* and published in *Charivari* for the 14th of March, 1834. It shows two young men and one old man in a prison cell. One of the younger men is reading to his companions from the *Tribune*. The coarse furnishings of the cell are shown in detail. The three men are said by Champfleury to be Daumier's companions in captivity, Lerouge, the engraver, Landon, the lawyer, and Masse, the writer of romance. The light and shade of the picture are sharply contrasted, the shining white jacket of the standing figure and the illumined wall back of the others giving an effect of great brilliancy to the whole. The modelling, however, is still a little soft, and lacks the decisive simplicity of other works even of the same year. One of these, which we reproduce, is the well-known *Rue Transnonain, Le 15 Avril*, 1834. In this powerful composition we see what Mr. McCall defines as Daumier's "grand and elemental" style, which, he says, is exercised upon trivial matter, but which in this instance is devoted to a subject that no critic, French or British, could condemn as "trivial." The scene is laid in one of the little side streets of the Saint-Martin quarter which are inhabited by workmen, and which were invaded by furious soldiery on one of the days of insurrection. A room has been entered, the furniture overturned, and the occupants slaughtered. Daumier has chosen the moment following the massacre. A deadly silence seems to pervade the place depicted. On the floor is lying a workman in a blood-stained shirt; under him a young child who has been crushed by his fall; at the right is an old man, and, in the background, near the door, a woman; both dead. The horror of such material is obviated for us only by the serene nobility of the method. Daumier is nowhere more completely the detached artist deeply moved by his subject, but unforgetful of the æsthetic rights of his art. As in the *Souvenir de Ste. Pélagie* he is as little as possible the satirist. The human situation has revealed its tragedy to him, and he treats it without exaggeration or whimsicality, and with a breadth and sombre splendour of style that accords with its significance.

Another drawing of 1834 is not less austere in its message but is in the vein of caustic irony. Louis-Philippe, in the company of a judge, is standing by the side of a co: on which lies a dying prisoner. Feeling his pulse, the king remarks, "This one may be set at liberty; he is no longer dangerous." Here again the execution is remarkable for its imposing simplicity and largeness. Although the forms are modelled with a sculptural solidity, they are set in an atmosphere that floats and shimmers—a circumambient air that fills the background with elusive mists. The fat hand of Louis extended in a gesture of explanation is a detail in which the later fluency of Daumier's line appears.

The *Rue Transnonain* drawing belongs to a set of five drawings, furnished by Daumier for a collection called *L'Association Mensuelle* which Philipon published. Another of the set is the famous one entitled *Le Ventre Legislatif*, in which thirty-five of the ministers and deputies of the Centre of 1834 are represented. It is a composition that seems to summarise Daumier's achievement in that divination of character upon which the success of the carica-turist must inevitably depend. The field abounded with types to which his pencil fitted itself as if by conscious compatibility. Louis-Philippe's reign was one in which Marseillaise fervour could find enough to condemn, and the people by whom he was surrounded lent themselves readily to the sarcasm of critics; especially of those critics who had in their own veins the fiery blood of Southern France; and to whom incessant compromise and the contradiction of high ideals by debased practices was fuel for an ever-burning flame of moral ardour in the cause of liberty.

As the historian of the bourgeois government Daumier has much to say to the student of French politics. Against the apostles of moderation and profitable peace he launched the arrows of his wit, not too sharply pointed, but none the less capable of inflicting ugly wounds. In the caricatures of this period much of the effect is due to the masterly psychological portraiture which interprets, without misrepresentation and even without any extraordinary emphasis, the inner qualities and moral features of the subject, precisely as the outer features are modelled with a terrible truth far more to be feared than the grossest exaggeration. It is interesting to recall that many of these portraits were made from little coloured clay models, in which Daumier revealed himself as to sculpture born, and nourished the tendency to be found in all his early work, the tendency to suggest high relief and to place an excessive emphasis upon what Mr. Berenson calls the "tactile values."

Of these clay models M. Geoffroy (writing in *L'Art et les Artistes* for June, 1905) says thirty-eight are in existence besides the statuette of *Ratapoil*, which has been cast in bronze, and the bas-relief of the *Emigrants*. Thirty-six of the portrait busts were at the time of writing in the possession of M. Philipon, the grandson of the Charles Philipon who founded *La Caricature* and *Charivari*, where Daumier's early drawings appeared, one of the remaining two was given to Champfleury, and the other to Nadar. The bas-relief of the *Emigrants* belongs to M. Geoffroy-

Dechaume, the son of the sculptor who was Daumier's
friend. Champfleury in this article is quoted as saying
that Daumier was present at the sessions of the Chamber of
Peers, a bit of clay in his hand, and modelled his portraits
from life, using them later as the basis for his lithographs.
M. Geoffroy-Dechaume, on the other hand, speaks of his
making the little busts "from life," but *immediately after*
leaving the Chamber of Deputies, which, of course, would
make them memory studies. Whatever the method, and
with an observation so acute and a memory so retentive
as Daumier's, such distinctions matter little, he arrived
at a result in which the salient characteristics of his subjects
were raised to the nth power without overwhelming their
natural appearance. M. Geoffroy, whose privilege it has
been to study the clay models in M. Philipon's collection
at first hand, says of them, as they now appear in their
damaged condition, with remnants of colour still clinging
to them: "Here in these glass cases, this exhibition of
little busts is particularly vengeful. It suggests a massacre
in which genius has not once missed its mark. Certain
resemblances, even, might be put aside and certain identi-
fications, without lessening the general appalling effect.
No doubt it is interesting to see Persil, the Attorney-General
with his straight sharp obstinate profile; Delessert, the
Préfet, with his bit of a nose and his baboon mouth; Jacques
Le Févre, the banker, with his face like a knife-blade;
Dubois d'Anger, the deputy and president of the Court of

Assizes, with his flesh, his thick neck and shoulders, and his chubby face; Chevandier, the deputy, with the double twist of his forelock and his trumpet nose; Guizot, minister, of an anxious physiognomy in which both ill-health and grief are recorded; Gallois, journalist, afflicted with hydrocephalus, whose small chin makes an extraordinary contrast with his large forehead; Viennet, deputy, academician, and fabulist, his head sunk in his stock, the bumps of his forehead looking as though he had been knocked about in some romantic brawl; Podenas, deputy, with his pointed forehead and his thick lip; Pataille, deputy, quite refined; Prunelle, deputy, physician, Mayor of Lyons, his scornful face partly hidden by his hair; d'Argout, minister, his chin poised on his cravat, his mouth and eyes artful, and his enormous nose like the beak of a *toucan;* Odier, banker and deputy, old, with a concentrated expression, his long white hair falling over his collar; Dupin the elder, president of the Chamber, all mouth, a huge mouth which pushes forward, fleshy and gaping, the lower part of the face heavy and surmounted by a low forehead with a pointed skull flanked by two vast ears; Barthe, Keeper of the Seals, Minister of Justice, moon-faced and tallow-complexioned; Charles de Lameth, deputy, converted to some, a renegade to others, with a discontented, peevish countenance, and a narrow head covered by the Church-warden's black skullcap; Fruchard, deputy, massive, bloated, his great nose hanging over his mouth, large cheeks, and no cranium;

Valout, deputy, anxious, pretentious, with a nose that
looks like a false one, and a bitter mouth; and Gady, judge
at Versailles, and Ganneron, deputy and candle merchant,
and Lecomte, and Delort, general and deputy—I follow,
for the most part, the labels edited by Champfleury.

"But I insist that the individual portrait is outrun and
that we find ourselves here in the presence of human types,
of forms and expressions which have such an interest as
to make unnecessary the putting of a name to the masks.
Caricature it may be, but a caricature that gives its value
to the dominant truth by these enormous noses, these
minute noses, these apologies for noses, these hollow or
drooping cheeks, these pointed or blunt skulls, these tightly
pressed or open mouths, these thin or thick lips which lock
in or pour forth their secrets, these thin or harsh smiles, these
fat smiles, these grins that deform the entire physiognomy
by their frightful bitterness, these heavy chins which hang
over their white cravats, chins that disappear in flesh and
goitrous growths, these heads almost without skulls, these
bald craniums, these white locks rolled into pigeon wings,
these flying white locks, these black locks plastered down
as if with wax, these red locks, these bits of white or black
whisker which frame red or yellow countenances, these
pallid, puffed, or emaciated faces, these eyes with red lids
and encircled with greenish rings, these round humid eyes
that leap from their sockets and seem about to roll down
the cheeks. Many of these visages make one think of

animals that growl, that grunt, that chew their cud, and that sleep, or of sick birds that weary on their perch. In truth they appear to be undergoing tortures, a prey to torments, gnawed by suffering, convulsed with grief. Moral maladies are added to physical defects, and their faces express with unusual violence their characteristic pretentiousness, self-importance, meanness, ill-temper: they are old beaux, sly accomplices, bourgeois burlesques, cruel ogres. And in spite of all there is good-nature and kindliness in Daumier's pitiless talent. He is ferocious, and he has the air of being so for fun. One certainly laughs, but the ferocity remains."

In the lithographs founded upon these models the good nature is more apparent than the ferocity. The bland charm of the medium has no doubt much to do with the fluent modelling, the modified outlines, the rich flow of the light and shade, but the difference lies chiefly in the fact that Daumier here was making his published statement, and his rare conscience would not permit him to put forth less than his full artistic power in these drawings by which his ability was to be represented. It was all very well to manipulate his bits of clay sufficiently to throw into violent relief the dominating feature of the physiognomy observed, but when it came to making a picture, the spirit of art swayed him as the spirit of satire could not, and the bitterness of his clay caricatures melted into the tenderness of closely related values, the beauty of fathomless shadows and caressing half-tones, the dignity of finely composed masses and free sweeping contours. Nevertheless, it is in this series of portraits of judges and lawyers that Daumier lays bare his ideal of justice and honesty with most force. His barristers delivering their arguments with shallow fury and conspicuous vanity arouse in one's mind an inevitable fervour of sympathy with dignity and quietude and candour. His judges, half-asleep or eager for the hour of release, inattentive or pompous, inspire not only a disgust for characters so unresponsive to high demands upon them, but also a more definite respect for the opposite type, fortunately known to most of us.

Le Charivari, a daily paper founded in 1832, also by Charles Philipon, received the larger number of Daumier's lithographs for nearly forty years. In this journal appeared between 1835 and 1839 the Robert Macaire series, the invention of which was claimed by Philipon. Robert Macaire, as Philipon perhaps conceived, and as Daumier indubitably realised him, is a rascal whose rascality has in it the dash and fire, the ebullience and picturesqueness of the Tartarin type. He is the prince of adventurers, impudent, insouciant, ready with wit and with tongue, making a million or a franc with equal complacency so long as he can make it by cheating; a master of tortuous sophistries, a promoter of empty schemes, the swindler of the stupid and the grasping. He leans back in his armchair, or struts about his office, his hands thrust impertinently under his coat-tails or plausibly gesticulating, his eyebrows insolently raised, his portly figure swelling with self-importance. He plays his game like a true French actor, absorbed in doing it as well as he can. He puts conscience into his deceptions and makes them passionately true to his ideal of a deception. There is something tremendous, regal, heroic in his scampish poses. The closely embroidered tissue of his invention is a rich surface that makes one think of the splendid fabrics of the Orient glittering with gold thread upon a groundwork of coarse cotton cloth. His victims are not less significantly characterised. Their greed matches his own. For the most part they are the poor and narrow creatures who pass through the world expecting much for nothing, and resenting a fate that has discriminated against them, however justly.

In these compositions, as in most of those involving political caricature, Daumier enters upon his task with such amplitude of insight, such thoroughness of interpretation that the sense of caricature drops from his work, leaving it brazen reality, showing its face quite shamelessly, almost innocently, and with no defect greater than the cruel caprice of nature has inflicted upon it, or might credibly have inflicted upon it.

When we arrive at the work undertaken in a gayer frame of mind with a more obvious joy in the pictorial possibilities of the scene, we find the lithographic chalk more frequently indulging in the entravagance of grotesque. In such a series as that of *Les Beaux Jours de la Vie*, that of *Types Parisiens*, or that of *Voyage en Chine*, there are occasional noses, mouths, or eyebrows for which one can find no parallel in commonplace experience. Even here, however, it is possible to observe one after another of the drawings without discovering a type that is not as familiar as the street through which one daily passes. An astute French critic recently has pointed out that Daumier frequently expressed his ideal by showing its opposite, that he emphasised his sense of beauty by displaying forms of ugliness that call up in contrast a mental vision of classic charm; that he emphasised his love of righteousness by holding vice up to ridicule; his love of integrity by setting forth the vulgarity of deception, and so on. This adroit analysis is certainly quite justified as far as it goes, and Daumier's passion for beauty is plausibly inferred from his keen eye for departures from it in our debased human physique. I recall a drawing belonging to the series called *Histoire Ancienne* in which *le beau Narcisse* is kneeling on the bank of a stream, regarding with delight his reflection in the water. The scrawny limbs, the awkward attitude, the large bullet head crowned with flowers, contradict all the features attributed to the classic conception. The figure is the cleverest of parodies, and has the hateful quality of the parody, in that it imposes itself upon the original, which henceforth we can see only in company with its distorted shadow. Daumier in this instance has yielded to a temptation altogether rare with

2

him. He has brought the sordid real in contrast with the imagined ideal without displaying the æsthetic possibilities of the former. His forms are cramped and his light and shade are distracted. In general, however, he exhausts every resource of reality from which æsthetic pleasure may be drawn, and his opulent supple line plays gaily over the most commonplace subjects, secure in its power to extract from them homage to the æsthetic ideal.

We have only to consider such a drawing as the one entitled *L'Odorat* to feel the full effect of the benignant point of view from which he regards the mere material ugliness of the physical world. An old peasant is leaning in night-cap and dressing-gown from a bedroom window to sniff the fragrance of a pot of flowers blooming on the sill. The homely plebeian head thrust out from the darkness of the room into the glow of the summer sunshine and modelled with large simplicity and freedom, the frame of common plants putting forth bright leaf and blossom in their coarse clay pots, the bird in his wooden cage, the pitcher hanging against the wall, making charming spots of decorative shadow, the rapturous upturned eyes, the clumsily sensitive hand spread in a caressing gesture—these supply an impression that epitomises the charm of humble joys simply taken; and only the most unimpressionable intelligence could fail to answer to both the sentimental and æsthetic appeal. The same genial tenderness in which amusement gleams without sharpness like a warm paternal smile is seen in the treatment of such physiognomies as that of *Le Chasseur Parisien*, who strolls through the thicket, his gun under his arm, placidly reading, while birds perch undisturbed on every side, a figure of vague abstraction, as appealing as a gentle child, or that of the illiterate old woman leaning on her broomstick and gazing skyward while her neighbour reads to her from the newspaper, with entire misinterpretation, the reports of her son's ship. Even the quaint papas and mamas whose unromantic visages are echoed in the features of their hideous offspring are depicted in the orthodox enjoyment of parental emotion with a discernment as free from irony as it is rich in philosophic wisdom, and with undisturbed attention to the artistic execution of the task. How lightly the artist's humour ran in harness with his sense of the beautiful is seen in perfection in his drawing of a little *bas-bleu* seated by an open window apostrophising the moon. She wears a scant gown and pulls at her under-lip with a graceless gesture, her large coarse hands and feet sprawling irresponsibly about; her common features and stupid expression proclaiming her the type of the pretentious dullard. The incongruity between her ideal and her actual makes an irresistible appeal to the spirit of mirth. Yet over her gaunt frame and ugly surroundings, and over her foolish face, the moonlight pours in such pale loveliness, with such refining charm, that the scene takes on an aspect independent of the satiric message it conveys. It becomes merely a drama in light and shade, and the *bas-bleu* falls in with the general enchanting effect as though she were one of the grimacing gargoyles on a Gothic Cathedral seen beneath the same fair moon. It is by such surrender to the spirit of beauty that Daumier continually wins us whether he amuses or fails to amuse.

Nevertheless, if in our appreciation of his sunny good-nature and of his readiness to clothe a ridiculous situation with all the charm of which his art is capable, we are oblivious of his well-defined intellectual attitude toward the small people of the world, we shall go far out of our path. His studies of bourgeois homes and bourgeois characters show clearly enough his detachment from their limited views and egoistic interests. The petty domain of a family without large ambitions or general ideas, without standards or measures of value, becomes under his scrutiny a laughable and also a more or less contemptible affair. He shows us with remorseless implication the complacency of mediocre citizens with their property, their pride in their stupid children, their satisfaction in their little fêtes and little occupations, their willingness to let the personal horizon everywhere shut out the wider view. In one of the lithographs which we reproduce a crowd of these good dull people are looking at the blossom of a night-blooming cereus, the extraordinary attributes of which are loudly proclaimed to them by a showman. In the craning heads, in the gaping mouths, in the vacant eyes, in the forced self-conscious wonder and admiration of the group we read without difficulty how superficial their sentiment is, how largely composed of a vulgar curiosity and desire merely to plume themselves upon having seen something that all the world does not see every day. For shams, innocent as they may be, Daumier has nothing but a scathing comment. His honest pencil unveils the foolish pretence and by the simple act seems to place the artist on that high plane of mental aristocracy where to be consciously superior or consciously exclusive is to be an alien. He is conspicuously an example of the attitude toward the bourgeoisie pointed out by Professor Wendell as characteristic of the French artist in any kind. Bourgeois himself in origin, he is also Bohemian and critical in temper of bourgeois manners and sentiments and of bourgeois limitations. He touches them, however, on their superficial side. The core of bourgeois virtue he treats with respect;—that is to say, he leaves it alone. But there are few of the mannerisms common to the undiscriminating mind that he allows to escape him; and it is in the portrayal of these that his mirth is most genial. Unceasingly severe with the counterfeit of real emotion, sentiment, or interest, he is gaily responsive to the minor joys of life as they come to the sober middle class. When we look at such a drawing as that bearing the legend: "C'est demain la fête de sa femme" ("To-morrow is his wife's birthday") it is easy to fancy the artist with his kind eyes and smiling mouth, strolling behind the devoted old husband who bends beneath the burden of floral decoration which he carries home for the great day, unconscious of the comment of the world outside his own.   We seem to note that Daumier saw first the humble figure carrying a couple of pots of flowering plants, that he thought to himself, "Now, who but a *bon bourgeois* would go through the streets like that.   Of course they are for his wife—happy lady—it doubtless is her birthday," that swiftly his prehensile vision added another flower-pot to the load and hung a napkin full of cut flowers to the weary arm, that in his mind's eye he saw the figure adapt its attitude to the heavier weight, and the picture was made, ready to be transferred to the page with just that little accent of excess that differentiates it from the scene as it appeared to every passer-by, and just that sweet sobriety of greys and soft blacks that makes the harmony in colour values appropriate to the sentiment inherent in the scene.

Kindred to this drawing in mildness of humour and suavity of execution are such others as *The Morning Pipe*, where the very atmosphere of placid dreams is evoked by the beautiful greys and whites through which the old smoker in night-cap and night-shirt, bolstered comfortably against his pillows, is made an object of æsthetic charm; the lovely drawing of an old bourgeois couple wandering homeward under a star-strewn sky to which they turn their vague fat faces with a sense of the scene's solemnity; the one entitled *L'Anniversaire du Mariage* in which M. and Mme. Coquelicot, with minds long attuned to material satisfactions, propose

to celebrate their thirty-first wedding anniversary by con-
suming a delicious turtle pie; that depicting the joy of one
of the readers of *Charivari* in unravelling a rebus published
therein, the victor hastening home to share his triumph with
his wife—all these and many others have the quality of
gentleness, they resemble a kind of pleasant gossip between
people of shrewd observation upon the subject of their
neighbour's activities. Not a touch of bitterness lurks in
the free comment, and we like the people themselves the
better for the light thus thrown upon them. The satire
in them, if satire is the name for mere notation of human
traits, is conveyed with the utmost subtlety without that
resource to the obvious which is the characteristic defect
of a low order of intelligence.

Daumier is not always so deft of thought. In his daily
supply of a daily demand for mirth-provoking art he
occasionally falls back upon the hackneyed shock to the
sensibilities given by the unexpected or the violently incongruous. One of the series entitled *Émotions Parisiennes*
(Parisian Sensations) shows a wrathful passer-by upon
whose head pots of flowers have fallen from a window-sill
above. The legend, which may or may not have been
Daumier's own, reads: "Life's road should be strewn with
flowers." Another of the same series presents to our sym-
pathies another unfortunate pedestrian struck in the face
by a great door or shutter which a workman is carrying.
The legend—"Ah! Excusez"—is refreshingly brief and

to the point after the many tedious ones with which Daumier's collaborators have provided his synthetic drawings.

Another depicts a "bon bourgeois" leaning out of his window to enjoy the summer breeze, and receiving upon his head the water from a window garden too copiously sprinkled by his neighbour on the floor above. Still another shows us a crouching figure overwhelmed by snow that has been shovelled upon it from the roofs, the sudden dip of the shoulders under the unexpected onslaught having a realism of movement such as only Daumier has succeeded in uniting to the "grand style."

These rather crude attacks upon our sense of the ludicrous serve chiefly, however, to mark the delicacies of others:— the private little shrug of cynicism, for example, that makes itself felt through the artist's comments upon the humdrum economies that pass before him. That "beau jour" upon which, according to the legend, "il faut se montrer galant" is one of mingled sweet and bitter for the absurd old gentleman too long unaccustomed to altruistic expenditure to meet courageously the demand for ten francs. He stands fingering the flowers at a stall, exclaiming in horror at their price. His coat of some antiquity, his features concentrated in painful calculation, the cool scorn of the hard-faced little flower vendor, the stiff propriety of the Parisian bouquets, the fine sun-besprinkled air of the handsome town circulating cheerfully through the soft shadows and luminous half-tones—what a real scene it is, how free from factitious feeling, how contemporary and definite, how charged with essential significance, and how profound in its casual criticism of human nature!

And in his light commentary on the terrors of weak souls to whom life is a panorama of dangers in ambush, how pleasantly his humour twinkles over the situation without pouring upon it too harsh a light! The frenzy of the wife plucking at her husband's coat as he looks down with alarming temerity upon a passing railroad train may have a certain surplusage of intensity; but what could be more completely within the boundaries of the natural than the expression of the nervous man who finally selects the coach he will travel in as he would cast a die at a gaming table, with a desperate dependence upon luck; or the haunted look of the little party of excursionists upon whom it has dawned that no accident has occurred upon the road for a number of days and the time of immunity must be drawing to an end; or the prophetic glare of the alarmist who knows there is to be a famine because his cook reports a rise in the price of whiting? Too comfortable in aspect to awaken pity, these honest, solemn sufferers at once appeal to our liking—we must love what so much amuses us.

Not infrequently Daumier resorts to the expedient of the expert moralist and sets down strongly contrasting types as he finds them without the slightest attempt at emphasising their differences, leaving us to divine for ourselves the conclusions indicated. Thus in the little drawing called

Ouvrier et Bourgeois (" Workman and Bourgeois ") of the series *Les Parisiens en 1848*—a drawing in which the secrets of the great masters are held by the modelled line and the serene architectonic composition that makes one think of temples and arches and classic vistas while noting the vitality of the contemporary figures—in this opposition of the work- man walking the street absorbed in the columns of his newspaper where must be recorded the stirring events of the revolution, to the stout gourmand equally absorbed in the display of luscious gustibles offered by a shop window, we have the simplest of sermons, the application of which is insisted upon only so far as the observer himself may choose to press the question.

And in the charming composition—so amusing, so tender, so delicate—entitled *Le Dimanche au Jardin des Plantes*, the "note" of reticence is even more admirably preserved, as though the artist after placing the little scene before us with his most ingratiating manner, drew back from it and said, "Now, let us find out what your powers of observation may be, dear public to whom I dedicate mine." Not that extraordinary powers are needed to discern the variations of type, once they are impressed upon the vision, but that the silvery tone enveloping the drawing holds so closely together the discriminated values, that the lines flow so quietly in one general direction, that the little procession moves along the sunlit path with a harmony upon which no sharp differentiation strikes discordantly, until the mind is cheated by the charmed eyes and the significance becomes clear only after a distinct intellectual effort. Then we see how the distinguished elderly man who advances with a subtle elegance of walk and bearing is faintly echoed by the figure at his left whose battered finery and sharp features are thus thrown into more eloquent contrast with the bland dignity of his neighbour. And passing by this quiet gradation to extremes of incongruity, we compare the fragile, aristocratic features of the little old lady, clinging to the arm of her companion, her eyes demurely bent, her lips modelled to a line of discreet reserve, her figure shrunken with years keeping its delicate elasticity, with the vulgar woman also clinging to her husband's arm but turning to gaze open-mouthed at the animals within the enclosure. The rude features, the flat foot, the short skirt showing loose stockings wrinkled upon heavy ankles, the indifferent hand clasped over that of the ugly little child who is pulled along by her side, the coarse outline all speak of that absence of intentional refinement, that ignorance of preconsidered daintiness, that disregard of particular detail which mark the plebeian standard of personal appearance.

This instruction by suggestion in the values of the social order betrays upon Daumier's part a finer instinct for social relations than that with which he commonly is credited. Bourgeois and Bohemian—so far as the latter is the inevitable state of the French artist—he may have been, but he was also to a degree patrician in his ultimate criticisms.

Without the taste for languid figures that gives to Gavarni's subjects a look of physical elegance, he separates with greater precision the qualities that depend upon external and those that depend upon inner delicacy. The democratic tendency which inspired his love of liberty and his scorn of those who assailed it openly or in secret was a deep-rooted sentiment, too vital and too intense to satisfy itself with the affectation of freedom implied by unrestrained manners. While for the most part he follows the tendency analysed by M. Gaultier and displays his appreciation of the mellifluous charm clinging to a social order founded upon high traditions and guarded seclusion by revealing the shuffle and clatter of a too democratic publicity, he is capable, as we see in the drawing just described, of penetrating the very temple of aristocracy and making its stillness, its exclusiveness, its fastidious felicity, apparent, without changing his own style for pitch of expressiveness, with a quietness equal to that of his subject and, too, with a feeling for the exquisite unsurpassed by any of his contemporaries.

When we turn to the subjects drawn from his own profession, it is interesting to note how his comic spirit sharpens. The air of good nature that softens the most caustic of his comments upon the world without drops as he enters his own domain. He unveils with a quite ferocious glee the pretentiousness of ignorant amateurs and casual buyers, and the stupidity of the vast public who throng the picture galleries. He depicts a sale at the Hotel Drouot with a crowd of eager bidders wisely inspecting an undecipherable canvas; he reproduces the flattered countenances of *bons bourgeois* who behold themselves in effigy on the walls of the salon and feel their money to have been well spent, the shrewder features of the patron who buys a second-hand portrait to have it touched up into his own likeness at a reduced rate, the haughty expression of the influential critic who passes through the galleries, notebook in hand, the indignant gesture of the Philistine who cannot be forced to admire a picture by Courbet. The logical visitor to exhibitions who wishes to know why the woman in Manet's picture of the year is called Olympia, and decides that it is the cat that bears the name; the conscientious visitor who discovers merits in dubious canvases by the aid of a magnifying-glass; the ardent lover of art who turns hastily away from the entrance door of the exhibition on finding that he has hit upon a pay-day; the self-sufficient visitor who finds fault with composition and colour with an air of authority—these appear in his lithographs clearly and coldly defined. On the other hand he is not less ready to put before us the painter who allows himself to take pleasure in ignorant praise, the painter who is content to copy fellow-artists in place of nature, and the one who panders to the vanity of his sitter.

It would be plausible to say, in spite of the instances noted of subtle characterisation and refined implication, that the examples of Daumier's art, chosen almost at random from the four thousand or so described in the catalogue, show, after all, as a whole, no supremely original vision, that the morals are for the most part commonplace, and that the wit is obvious. They are made, it is easy to see, for the every-day public. They represent familiar scenes and figures in a way to claim immediate recognition if not immediately to convey their intellectual message,—that is the *sine qua non* of the caricaturist's trade. Even if they have the subtlety of feeling that is claimed for them they have a bluntness and completeness of expression that contrasts sharply with the abstract outline of a Caran d'Ache. They come into the presence of more modern caricature as the burly form of an elderly farmer might enter a dapper society of some one of the great cities of the world. They have about them an atmosphere of incorrigible innocence and solid worth that is not of modernity or for that matter of any time or place, that is purely an individual envelope. For the most part they are jovial and outspoken, they have mental energy and a spontaneous exuberance. They are not mysterious or alluring. They are oftener gay than sad. They are always agreeably confidential, taking the observer into their secret at once and assuring him that he knows all there is to know. But they are nevertheless, like Joey Bagstock, sly—deep and sly in their wealth of reserve quality. They wear their plainness on their sleeve, resembling some old miser who goes about in homespun with a pot full of gold in his cellar. They are perfectly exemplified in the story told of Daumier himself by Champfleury, who says that he once passed an entire night with a body of national guards who failed to have the least suspicion that their companion was a dangerous observer upon whom nothing was lost. Beneath the bonhomie of his large, free style, his magnificent simplicity, are hidden treasures of observation for the assiduous student who frequents the lithographs in a sympathetic mood. Their scope is almost that of the human comedy; intimate scenes of home life classified, as *Mœurs Conjugales*, *Les Papas*, *Scénes de Famille*, *Scénes Conjugales*, etc.; scenes of Bohemian Paris, of bourgeois Paris, of political Paris, scenes of the changing seasons with their various occupations and amusements, of passing social phases, of financial situations legitimate and fantastic; quaint criticisms on administrative manners, such as are grouped under the title *Le Voyage en Chine*, studies of the stage and of the studios, portraits of judges and barristers, of strong-minded women, of musicians and butchers, of philanthropists and tyrants, of soldiers and huntsmen, householders and servants. The principal phase omitted is that of the ballroom. Among the two or three hundred of Daumier's works that I have seen I recall but one that leads even to the door of a fashionable entertainment. This one commemorates the announcement of a newly ennobled personage by the servant, as "M. le Ba-aron Bois-flotté."

His society passes its time chiefly out-of-doors, in the public parks, and on the city streets, or in the living-rooms of simple homes in which behaviour is marked by great regularity. Indiscretions of conduct form but a small part of his baggage as a chronicler of the passing show. He portrays family life largely on the side of its devotions, and by his merciless rendering of the infant physiognomy he appears to assure us that no child exists too unattractive to win the fatuous commendation of its parents. His fathers, in particular, sacrifice to their offspring. When he shows us the night on which the child is wakeful ("une nuit agitée") the father is seen kneeling before the fire warming flannels for it; he shows us many times over the father who instructs his son in the art of swimming, one delightful plate in particular, in which the artist has given rein to his love of things as they are, is that portraying with unsparing realism the child clinging crab-like to the father's neck and distorting his features by howls of terror. There are other scenes in which similar swimming lessons go more smoothly; he shows us the father who escorts his children home from their school on the day of the distribution of prizes, the children wearing crowns of flowers and decorations, the father alone without award of merit. "This really is unfair," the legend affirms. He shows us the father who enhausts his lungs blowing the fleet of his infant son to sea; the father who jumps rope with his son and daughter; the one who plays horse. He shows us fathers and mothers together reflecting

with delight upon the superiority of their little ones who
gaze out at us with innocently afflicting faces.   He shows
us the fine deeds of these little ones who compose poetry
for the birthday of Papa, who suck barley sugar-sticks
"with such an air," who walk with a style that forecasts
important careers for them.   All this without the slightest
indication of ill-feeling toward the little men and women who
lend themselves so obligingly to a rollicking pencil.   In the
plate belonging to the series *Locataires et Propriétaires*
("Landladies and Tenants") where the mother, holding by
the hand a meek-faced boy of three or four years, endeavours
to obtain rooms from an old woman surrounded by animals
who replies, "I do not let to people with children," the
opposite point of view is sufficiently implied.

As one follows Daumier's work with reference to its
artistic development, from his early and feeble drawings
through the magisterial portraits of Louis Philippe's reign
to the more varied record of passing events and social types,
one perceives a steady growth of the quality least often
found in connection with a monumental style—the sense of
movement.   In all the later lithographs nothing is more
salient than this.   The energy of motion is in every line
of the men and women and children, of the dogs and cats
and horses—nothing is fixed or posed, everything is ready
to shift and change as in a Japanese drawing of the Ukiyo-ye
school.   In the later work, too, there is a closer relation than
in the earlier between the shadows or lights and the middle

tones. The whites are not less white—Daumier has to the
end a fondness for broad patches of the pure unsullied ground
of white paper which gleams in a shirt-front, a night-cap,
a blouse, a table-cloth, an apron, or a broad stretch of
blank wall; but the greys are higher in key as they approach
the highest light and where the proportion of dark is greatest
in a drawing there is more of the low-toned grey, so that the
forms are relieved with less violence against their background. In the modelling of flesh there is a finer sense of
the variations of surface, the local colour of different parts
of the face also receives a singularly exact translation into
terms of black and white; the texture of fabrics, of glass
and wood, of hair and fur, are differentiated with a closer
precision, and especially the envelope of air becomes more
pervasively felt. In a word, as Daumier continued practis-
ing his art with the spontaneity and freedom required of
a contributor to the daily press he became more and more
an artist—the world appealed to him more and more on its
purely pictorial side. During the decade between 1849
and 1860 he seems, according to M. Delteil, to have lan-
guished somewhat at his task, executing his drawings of
that period with a too summary method, and showing a
certain lack of the intensity of interest always previously
to be found in his work, of however slight a character it
might be. In 1860, according to the current tradition, he
decided to quit *Charivari* and abandon lithography for
painting; but according to a statement made by Philippe

Burty and transcribed by M. Delteil, he became at this time unpopular with the magazines which formerly had relied upon his support and *Charivari* declined to renew its contract with him. Whatever the exact cause, he did at this period turn to painting and produced water-colours and oils as remarkable in their kind as his drawings in theirs. I have seen the originals of only a few of these paintings, but the ones owned by Mr. Cyrus J. Lawrence of New York, Sir William van Horne of Montreal, and Mr. John G. Johnson of Philadelphia are of an authority, a homogeneity, and an amplitude of style sufficient to prove his place among the masters of painting. The more we study him the more we realise that his simplicity of workmanship is made up of many contributions from sources of great variety; his simplicity of character is perhaps the unifying element that made even his rich perception of the incongruous a beneficent tool in his hands rather than a destructive weapon.

M. Prune

(37)

Robert-Macaire, a Banker after the Style of the Turks:

"The news cannot be known at Bordeaux; take the post, ride ten horses to death, arrive ahead of everyone, sell short and we shall realize at least a million. I, meanwhile, will go to the palace; we are condemning this morning a scamp who stole ten francs,—ten francs!— the b-b-blackguard!"

The Red-Letter Days of Life.

A Delicate Attention.

"How do you like this shawl, my dear?   I chose it myself."
"Charming, lovely, but I had no need of that to love you, dear
Edward!"

(41)

"Sorry, my good woman, but I don't carry dogs in my 'bus."
"Aristocrat, begone!"

(43)

Robert-Macaire, Commission-Agent

"How the devil is this, Sir, you say you pay only on Saturdays, and this is the third Saturday that I have come for a bill of nine francs, fifty centimes, and I am never able to get it!"

"You come too early, the bank is not open till three o'clock."

"Very well! It is a quarter past three now."

"It is too late, the bank closes at precisely three o'clock. Deuce take it, my dear Sir, it is all your own fault, you should be exact—come on the hour."

(45)

"Yes, my pet, it is more than three weeks since this poor dear man has swallowed a mouthful. I have just made him a good little cabbage soup with the lard gravy which he likes so much and some potatoes; those doctors would soon have him dead of hunger with their dieting."

Parisian Types

"Don't say a word, I have such a cold in the head that I can't see
out of my eyes, my dear!"

(49)

Parisian Types.

"You reason like a sugar-cane!"
"And you like a beet!"

(51)

"See him strut with such a style—you'd swear he was an officer of the artillery, and that he was cut out for a great lawyer or powerful business man."—(*Conjugal Habits.*)

(53)

Silhouettes.

The Care-Taker.

So called, by antithesis, because she neither takes care of the furniture, nor of the china, nor of the wine of her employers.

Bohemians of Paris

The Marauder

Mr. Minet, general contractor for Parisian rabbit-stews (Dinners for
32 sous)

"Come—come—come—come along my rabbit!"

Parisian Types.

The annoyance of talking with people who have a mania for putting their words into action: " Yes, my dear sir, would you believe that the b-blackguard permitted himself to laugh in my face? You know that I have not a temper that will stand everything. So I clutched him—so—and shook him—so—vigorously!"

Bohemians of Paris.

The Sick-Nurse.

"There is no one like the fruiterers to get you nice cases. An epileptic
and hydrophobic patient and one lunatic. Now if the grocer gets the
consumptive he promised I shall be well fixed."

(61)

Events of the Day.
Subscribers trying to read their papers.

The Red-Letter Days of Life.

The Illustrated Rebus.

" Singular!   I cannot guess the rebus in to-day's *Charivari* ! "
" I think I have one word—I have several words—I have it all—I am
going home to tell my wife ! "

(65)

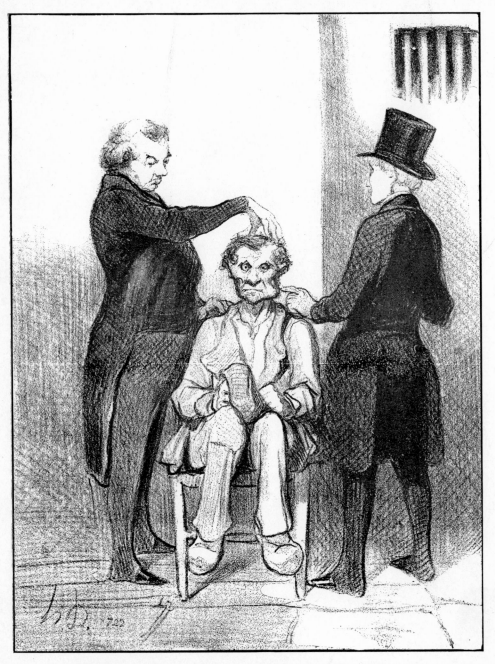

"Monsieur is a great thief? That's all right. I hope to correct that with the aid of my system. It is impossible to reform a man if one does not pay the greatest attention to his protuberances. Everything depends on that."

"Say, then, there is a famous one on the cheek."

(The Prisoner) "Pay no attention to that, gentlemen,—it's a chaw of tobacco."

(67)

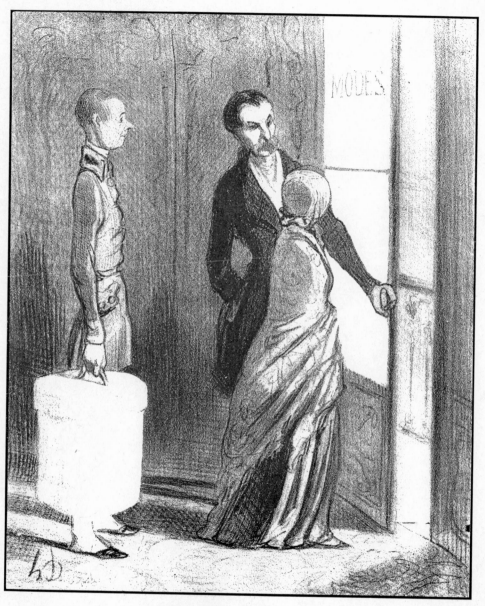

The Philanthropists of To-Day.

Monsieur Mimi Coquet, milliner and philanthropist, in order to save young girls the dangers they might run in carrying a hat-box on the sidewalk, discharges them.

The Red-Letter Days of Life.

A Nomination.

"Tell me, Sir,—are you nominated at last?"
"Yes, 'Supernumerary Aspirant'—and I am informed that there are
only eighty-seven ahead of me."

(71)

Friends.

A friend is a crocodile given to us by civilization.

(73)

The Red-Letter Days of Life.

A Visit to the Studio.

"I am going to send it at once to the Louvre—I think it will make something of an impression!"

"It is cha-a-aming—it is cha-a-aming!"

(75)

The Red-Letter Days of Life.

A New Member of the Nobility.

(The servant, announcing) "The Ba-aron Driftwood!"

The Red-Letter Days of Life.

The Wedding Anniversary.

" It is actually thirty-one years ago to-day, Monsieur Coquelet ! "
" True! We must celebrate this memorable day. Let us go eat a
turtle-pie with force-meat. "

The Red-Letter Days of Life.

Carnival Time.

"Let us go laugh and caper! I shall be disguised as a clever rogue."
"Fine! No one will recognize you!"

(81)

The Instructor:
"Your son does me honour!—he is a charming subject!"

(83)

The Papas.

"Ah! sir, don't laugh like that, you will make him cry!"

(85)

When one has bad luck—

"The deuce!   Full!"

(87)

"I present to you my son Théodule, just out of college and already with a crowd of victims—all the young ladies wish to marry him."

"The scamp!—he takes after his father!"

Travels in China.

A Milliner's Shop.

One fine day a crowd of young women in China took it into their heads to claim the rights of man, and immediately a number of men profited by the occasion to usurp the occupations of women. In the Imperial Capital, especially; only male shirtwaist-makers, dress-makers, milliners, etc., etc., are seen at Pekin, where already people are somewhat accustomed to these ways and to these rude faces, but foreigners who enter these curious shops cannot help exclaiming: "Ah! what queer creatures Chinamen are!"

(91)

The Universal Exposition.

View of the Exposition at three P.M. on a sunny day; 86 degrees in the shade!

(93)

The Universal Exposition.
Fabrics that are positively waterproof.

(95)

Opening of the Hunt.

A Parisian who is not accustomed to encounter wild animals.

(97)

Events of the Day

"Polichinelle, Polichinelle,—you have cudgelled others long enough—
it's your turn now—you are going to be taught reason."

(99)

The Universal Exposition.
The Department of Clocks.

(101)

The Railways.

"They go at an infernal rate with their devilish engines—when will a benefactor of humanity arrive to reinvent the stage coach!"

(103)

The Universal Exposition.

A Family Luncheon.

(105)

The Railways.

"Well, here's to good luck! Perchance in this one we will be free from accident!"

Winter Sketches.

On the way to taste what one is pleased to call, even in the month of December, the pleasures of the chase!

(109)

Summer Sketches.

"I do indeed wish to learn to swim, but not in the water, papa,—oh!
not in the water!"

(111)

"My dear sir, I will gladly pay another franc if you will have the very
great kindness to get me out of this turnstile."

(113)

Parisian Sketches.

They Day for the Distribution of Prizes.

A Parisian bourgeois, no matter who, escorting his children home from some school, no matter what one.—The father alone is not crowned and it is verily unjust.

(115)

Events of the Day

Impressions of Railway Travel

"It is already eight days since there has been an accident on this line—
it can't last long—I am sorry we took this excursion train."

(117)

Events of the Day.

"Come back, my dear, I beg—the railroads have been so dangerous of late that an accident might happen to you just looking at a passing train."

(119)

The Railways.

Third-class travellers—completely frozen.

(121)

Events of the Day.

A Dream that Turns to Reality.

Seeing himself forced to swallow the broth which Peter the Great has prepared for him.

(123)

The Pleasures of the Chase.

Behold what one is in the habit of calling the lively emotions of the chase!

(125)

Aquatic Sketches

"Enter the water without fear Mr. Potard, you see there is no danger, as I am already in it!"

"Madame Potard, if you had read Buffon you would be less bold—you would know that two of the most terrible animals in nature are in the ocean—sharks and lobsters!"

(127)

Events of the Day.
The Awakening of Italy.

(129)

At the St. Maur Encampment.

Visit to the tents of the Zouaves.

"Look, they sleep like ordinary men."

(131)

Our Troopers.

In Italy.

"Great Scott! one must eat his soup quickly in this country—the longer one waits the hotter it gets!"

(133)

Summer Sketches
View of the Entrance to the Deligny Baths

(135)

At the St. Maur Encampment.

M. Prudhomme satisfying a warlike fancy for camping in a Zouave's tent.

(137)

In China.

The American Ambassadors arrived at Pekin.

(139)

In China.

"Look at that box—it contains the American envoys on the way to Pekin!"

"Any one would say it was a coach full of curious animals."

"Faith! If they are curious, so much the worse for them, for they can't see much of the country they are travelling through."

(141)

Sketches of the Hunt

"Look, I have just killed a magnificent grouse!"

"Unlucky dog! It is the Brahma rooster from the neighbouring farm—a rooster that may cost you over thirty sous—to say nothing of the drubbing you 'll get."

(143)

In China

Chinese Patrol Reconnoitring

(145)

Events of the Day.

China Civilising Herself.

"Now, attention! this is the European theory—the eyes fifteen feet in front and bring the foot that is on the ground up to meet the one that is in the air."

(147)

In China.

"Tchinn-Tchinn, you bring good news! I accord to you the signal
honour of kissing the august dust of my august slippers!"

(149)

Events of the Day.

"See, Adelaide, I wished to give you a surprise—I have brought these Zouaves to dine with us—four men and a corporal!   I warn you they have good appetites!"

(151)

Events of the Day.

More wonders of the magnetising stone—or how, in society, to make ladies take poses no less fatiguing than ungraceful.

(153)

Events of the Day.

"To think that we are now Parisians!"

(155)

The World Depicted.
Photographers and Photographed.

(157)

Dramatic Sketches by Daumier

"Ah! my dear Sir, you have given me a delightful evening. You reminded me of Talma."

"Truly did I remind you of Talma?"

"Yes, especially in the shape of your nose."

Events of the Day.
European Equilibrium.

(161)

Events of the Day

Charivari obliged to make at short notice a new picture of the place
where the Temple of Peace is erected.

(163)

Events of the Day.

"Ow, ow, he has licked the butter off my bread."

(165)

Events of the Day.

At Clichy.

Asking himself if the abolition of imprisonment for debt will be
ratified in time to let him go to the Exposition.

(167)

Events of the Day.

Regretting that they are not millers.

(169)

Events of the Day.

The one who looks to the South: The Deuce!
The one who looks to the East: The Dickens!

(171)

Events of the Day.

What England calls *a trait-d'Union*.

(173)

Events of the Day.
With apologies to the Japanese.

(175)

Events of the Day
A Laureate in 1868

(177)

Events of the Day.
What the deuce is taking away his appetite?

(179)

Events of the Day.

The Prince of Hohenzollern finds the approach decidedly too grim.

(181)

Events of the Day

' What the dickens are they doing up there?"

(183)

Events of the Day.

"My fields pillaged, my horse carried off, my money stolen, that is
what they call patriotic!"